T0379028

TEEN CULTURE

▶

Across the Generations

Naomi Rockler

ReferencePoint
Press

San Diego, CA

About the Author

Naomi Rockler is an educational freelance writer who writes nonfiction and fiction books for teens. She lives in Minnesota with her husband and daughter.

© 2025 ReferencePoint Press, Inc.
Printed in the United States

For more information, contact:
ReferencePoint Press, Inc.
PO Box 27779
San Diego, CA 92198
www.ReferencePointPress.com

Picture Credits:
Cover: Shutterstock

6: Jacob Lund/Shutterstock
9: Camarique/Alamy Stock Photo
13: Beatriz Vera/Shutterstock
17: Nicole Glass Photograph/Shutterstock
19: Sally and Richard Greenhill/Alamy Stock Photo
23: Robert Landau/Alamy Stock Photo
25: Carlos Barquero/Shutterstock

29: Tracksimages.com/Alamy Stock Photo
33: Shanna Madison/TNS/Newscom
35: Ben Houdijk/Shutterstock
38: Mira/Alamy Stock Photo
40: Shawshots/Alamy Stock Photo
44: Stokkete/Shutterstock
48: Underwood Archives/UIG/Bridgeman Images
50: ClassicStock/Alamy Stock Photo
54: Hurricanehank/Shutterstock

LIBRARY OF CONGRESS CATALOGING-IN-PUBLICATION DATA

Names: Rockler, Naomi, author.
Title: Teen culture across the generations / by Naomi Rockler.
Description: San Diego, CA : ReferencePoint Press, Inc., 2025. | Includes bibliographical references and index.
Identifiers: LCCN 2024038743 (print) | LCCN 2024038744 (ebook) | ISBN 9781678210106 (library binding) | ISBN 9781678210113 (ebook)
Subjects: LCSH: Teenagers--Social life and customs--Juvenile literature. | Teenagers--Social conditions--Juvenile literature. | Popular culture--Juvenile literature.
Classification: LCC HQ796 .R6225 2025 (print) | LCC HQ796 (ebook) | DDC 305.235--dc23/eng/20240905
LC record available at https://lccn.loc.gov/2024038743
LC ebook record available at https://lccn.loc.gov/2024038744

CONTENTS

Teen Culture: Today and in the Past

"I have slumber parties with my friends where we eat snacks and talk about boys and post embarrassing photos," says Caroline, a sixteen-year-old from New Hampshire. "I wear small clothing. I wear obscenely oversized clothes. I put glitter on my face and shout cheers with kids I barely know at sports games and pep rallies."[1]

What Caroline is describing is her personal experience with teen culture, which refers to the ways that teens of a particular era express themselves, make sense of the world, have fun, and form connections with peers. Teen culture includes music, leisure activities, fashion trends, slang, movies and television, and social media.

Teens from years past explored their identities in similar ways. As writer Tom Rodriguez recalls about the 1950s, "It was all about being young, of being a part of a social revolution, being exposed to great new music, learning about girls, buying my first car, and experiencing all of it with my friends and the young people who lived in my hometown of Topeka, Kansas."[2] Similarly, Christine, a teacher from Texas, recalls the 1980s. "I spent my days riding my bike around the neighborhood being carefree and coming home before dark," she writes. "I would rush home from school to throw my backpack on the floor and put my Madonna record onto the record player."[3]

For young people today, teen culture is different than it was for their parents or grandparents. However, although tastes and attitudes change, there are ways that teen culture stays the same. Most importantly, teen culture is a big part of how teens develop identities separate from their parents and explore who they want to be.

Inventing the Teenager

The concept that teenagers are a distinct demographic group only dates back to the 1940s. "Humans have been turning 13 for tens of thousands of years," explains journalist Derek Thompson, "but only recently did it occur to anybody that this was a special thing, or that the bridge between childhood and adulthood deserved its own name."[4]

Several factors contributed to the modern definition of the teenager. The first was mandatory education, which did not exist before the twentieth century. By 1945, most states required students to attend school until they were sixteen. This meant that for the first time, large numbers of young people spent their days together. Another factor was widespread car ownership in the 1950s. Cars gave teens the freedom to socialize, date, and have separate lives from their parents.

> "Humans have been turning 13 for tens of thousands of years, but only recently did it occur to anybody that this was a special thing, or that the bridge between childhood and adulthood deserved its own name."[4]
>
> —Derek Thompson, journalist

In addition, starting in the 1940s, advertisers deliberately promoted the idea that teenagers were a distinct demographic group. By doing so, they were able to directly market things to teens, including movies, television shows, and clothing. During the post–World War II economic boom, many teens had discretionary cash, and advertisers wanted to capitalize on this. In fact, the term *teenager* did not become popular until advertisers started using the word in print in the 1940s.

Teen Culture: A Brief History

Most of the grandparents of today's teens were born after World War II and are referred to as *baby boomers*. They were teens between the 1950s and early 1980s. At the beginning of this era, teens were expected to conform to conservative social norms, including traditional gender roles. Frustrated with conformity, many rebelled by listening to rock and roll music. This rebellious spirit exploded during the 1960s. Teens listened to music that questioned the status quo, like psychedelic rock and folk music. Many teens were involved in Vietnam War protests and the civil rights movement.

Most of the parents of today's teens grew up in the 1980s (a group sometimes called Generation X) or the 1990s (a group known as millennials). This was an era when children and teens tended to be unsupervised by their parents. Teens listened to vibrant pop music, with icons such as Madonna, Prince, and Cyndi

Teen culture *is a term used to describe the way teens express themselves, make sense of the world, and form connections with their peers.*

Lauper. They expressed themselves through colorful fashions like neon colors and acid-washed jeans. Teens in the 1990s dressed in more understated ways, like flannel shirts, and listened to eclectic music that included grunge, hip hop, and electronic dance music.

Teen Culture Today

Today's teens are known as Generation Z (born between 1997 and 2012) or Generation Alpha (born after 2012). Technology and social media have become a huge part of teen culture. Because of streaming services and YouTube, teens have access to a vast library of music, television programs, and movies. Many teens are more politically aware and frightened about the future than their parents were as teens. In addition, today's teens are more diverse than other generations and have been raised with norms that are more inclusive and accepting.

Teen culture today is a work in progress. What future generations will learn about the teens of the 2020s remains to be seen.

CHAPTER ONE

Changing Attitudes, Changing Times

As teens grow up, they learn from their families, teachers, peers, and popular culture what is considered "normal" behavior and what is not. These lessons about cultural norms impact many aspects of teen life, including how teens dress, socialize, date, and treat people who are different from them.

At the same time, although teen culture reflects the worldview of teens' parents and society, it sometimes challenges this worldview. After all, an important part of being a teen is developing an identity separate from one's parents. Throughout the years, teens have challenged dominant attitudes through their dress, music, social activism, and other aspects of teen culture.

Attitudes About Gender Roles

According to Planned Parenthood, the nation's leading provider of reproductive health care and sex education, gender roles are rules about "how we're supposed to act, speak, dress, groom, and conduct ourselves based upon our assigned sex."[5] During the 1950s, gender norms were rigid. Many women were expected to marry young and stay home with their children. Television programs such as *Father Knows Best* (1954–1960) portrayed idyllic (and White) families in which men were in charge.

Teen culture largely reflected these gender roles. Fashion was traditional: boys had buzz cuts and jeans, and girls had neatly coiffed hair and modest skirts. Schools enforced these norms. "In my high school in the 1960s we were finally able to convince the administration that it would be alright for girls to wear slacks to school, slacks mind you, not jeans," recalls Karen Osburn, who grew up in New York during the 1960s. Osburn says few girls participated in sports back then. "There was only one girl on the cross country team in my senior year," she remembers, "and since she was better than some of the boys they were not happy about that."[6]

In the 1960s and 1970s, gender roles became less rigid. The women's liberation movement began and advocated for gender equality. More women went to college and entered the

This photo from 1954 shows two teens walking home from school. Most teen fashion from this time was conservative, with boys often wearing jeans and girls wearing modest skirts.

workforce. Teen culture reflected these changes. Boys grew their hair long, and girls wore jeans and miniskirts. More girls participated in sports.

Gender Roles in the 1980s and 1990s

The parents of today's teens grew up with mixed messages about gender. Women in the workplace became commonplace. But at the same time, many working women were still expected to take charge of the housework and child care—an inequitable standard that contributed to the high divorce rate during this era.

Teens also experienced mixed messages. On the one hand, more girls participated in sports, and boys participated in activities like art and music. Colorful gender-neutral clothing was popular—as reflected by pop artists such as Boy George, David Bowie, and Prince, who dressed in gender-fluid ways. On the other hand, women and girls felt pressure to conform to unforgiving beauty standards, especially about weight. The female beauty ideal became much thinner, peaking in the 1990s with a dangerously thin look known as "heroin chic," an emaciated look that resembled the appearance of a drug addict. Girls went on diets at young ages, and eating disorders skyrocketed. Popular shows such as *Beverly Hills, 90210* portrayed girls with both looks and lifestyles that were unattainable. "Television, movies, and *Seventeen* magazine taught me that the teenage dream meant having the nicest clothes, the clearest skin, shiniest hair, biggest house, and hanging at all the best parties,"[7] writes author Heather Cumiskey, who was a teen during the 1980s.

> "Television, movies, and *Seventeen* magazine taught me that the teenage dream meant having the nicest clothes, the clearest skin, shiniest hair, biggest house, and hanging at all the best parties."[7]
>
> —Heather Cumiskey, an author who grew up in the 1980s

Teens and Gender Roles Today

Today, social media has magnified pressure for girls to meet rigid beauty standards. As journalist Anna North writes, "Where once beauty standards were enforced by a handful of magazines and

Mental Hygiene Films

In the 1950s, many adults were nervous that teens were starting to resist the conformist norms of the day. In response, educators created a school staple: the mental hygiene filmstrip. Shown in classrooms, these short films showed young (almost always White) actors demonstrating the "correct" way to behave. For younger kids, there were films about how to behave in the lunchroom and how to appreciate one's parents. For teens, there were films about how to behave on dates. In *What to Do on a Date* (1950), a narrator teaches Nick how to ask a girl out and warns him not to kiss her goodnight on a first date. In *More Dates for Kay* (1952), Kay demonstrates how to get a boy to ask her out: by grooming herself well and asking boys for help with her homework. Other films taught teens that popularity and fitting in is very important. In the 1960s, mental hygiene films warned teens not to smoke marijuana. To modern audiences, these films seem laughably preachy and badly written—and, in fact, many kids at the time felt the same way.

consumer brands, that enforcement has now been outsourced to individual users of Instagram and TikTok, who have more than filled the void of 'aspirational' images that require extensive body modification to achieve."[8]

However, for teens today, gender role expectations are different than they were for their parents and grandparents. Teens have grown up in a world with stay-at-home dads and female scientists and basketball stars. In fact, teen culture is challenging the concept of gender itself and the long-held belief that there are two distinct genders. Many teens identify as nonbinary, gender fluid, or transgender. "Gen Z speaks a whole language of gender often barely understood by their Gen X and even Millennial parents,"[9] says psychology professor Jean M. Twenge.

> "Gen Z speaks a whole language of gender often barely understood by their Gen X and even Millennial parents."[9]
>
> —Jean M. Twenge, psychology professor

Attitudes About Inclusion and Diversity

In the 1950s and 1960s, racism was common. In most of the South, Black people were considered second-class citizens. Segregation was mandated by law in schools, neighborhoods, pools, restaurants, and public bathrooms. In the North, many schools and neighborhoods were also segregated, although not by law, and many White people were openly racist.

This racism impacted teen culture. Even in integrated schools, cross-racial social interaction was often limited. But at the same time, many teens of all races participated in the civil rights movement in the 1950s and 1960s. In addition, music opened doors toward integration. As the Digital Public Library of America explains, "Rock and roll appealed to teenagers from many backgrounds, and rock concerts often hosted mixed-race audiences. White teenagers embraced the music of African American musicians like Little Richard, Fats Domino, and Chuck Berry, while African American teenagers listened to white rock and rollers, such as Elvis."[10]

Overall, inclusion and diversity were not valued during this period. LGBTQ people were vilified and faced violence. Religious minorities had little visibility outside their own communities. Disability rights were virtually nonexistent until the 1970s.

Inclusion and Diversity in the 1980s and 1990s

Many of the parents of today's teens attended integrated high schools, with interracial friendships and dating. Television and movies became less monocultural, and shows about Black families, such as *The Cosby Show* (1984–1992), became popular.

At the same time, racist humor and exclusionary language were common, including fat jokes, homophobic slurs, and the use of the word *gay* as a synonym for *bad*. This was echoed in popular culture. An egregious example was the popular teen film *Sixteen Candles* (1984). In addition to its homophobic slurs, the film includes a cartoonishly stereotypical Asian character named Long Duk Dong. As pop culture writer Chris Lane explains, "A gong is sounded in the background when he appears, he pronounces Rs as Ls, and he's a caricature of Asian males who seems to be interested only in sex. He's one cruel Asian joke after another."[11]

In the 1990s, this kind of insensitive language was called out by a movement on college campuses that sought to promote inclusivity. Not everyone supported this movement, which some criticized as a form of social censorship they called "political correctness." Regardless, this movement brought widespread awareness to diversity issues, which carried over into the next generation.

Inclusion and Diversity for Today's Teens

In some parts of America, attitudes about diversity and inclusion are similar to those from the past. Critics dismiss diversity initiatives as "woke" censorship efforts. In some schools, teachers are forbidden or discouraged from teaching about slavery and racism. LGBTQ students at these schools often receive little support.

Nonetheless, as a whole, today's teens live in a world that values diversity far more than when their grandparents were teens. This is in part because of the diversity of teens themselves. According to a 2022 Pew Research Center report, only 52 percent of Americans born after 1996 are White, compared to 70 percent of Americans born between 1965 and 1980 and 82 percent born between 1946 and 1969. Moreover, about 20 percent of teenagers identify as LGBTQ, which is a dramatic difference from their

Attitudes about gender and diversity have changed dramatically for teens. More than 20 percent now identify as LGBTQ, compared to in the past when very few LGBTQ teens revealed their identities.

grandparents' generations, in which few LGBTQ teens revealed their identities. "You can identify as whatever," says Nadia Mc-Claflin, an Iowa high school student. "I think it's normal, at least in our school. I have straight friends, gay friends, bi friends, pan friends."[12]

Attitudes About Sex

Just as attitudes about gender and diversity have changed dramatically since the 1950s and 1960s, so have attitudes about sex. According to a 1963 Roper poll, only 19 percent of men and 17 percent of women thought sex before marriage was acceptable, even between engaged couples. In contrast, a 2022 Gallup poll found that 71 percent of Americans approve of sex outside of marriage.

Despite these attitudes, unmarried people—including teens—had sex in the 1950s. Culture writer Gabrielle Glaser argues that teens "had unsupervised time and space in the expanding new

Changing Religious Attitudes in America

Since the 1950s, one of the biggest changes in American life has been the importance of religion—especially Christianity—in the lives of many Americans. Although Christianity is still the dominant religion in the United States, fewer people are Christians. According to a 2022 Pew Research Center report, 90 percent of Americans were Christians in 1973. In 2020, that number was down to 63 percent, including only 54 percent of teens between the ages of fifteen and nineteen. In 1973, only 5 percent of Americans were unaffiliated with any particular religion; in 2020, 29 percent were unaffiliated, including 39 percent of teens. About 10 percent of teens consider themselves atheist or agnostic—beliefs that were mostly taboo in the 1950s.

In addition, today's teens live in a culture in which religious inclusivity is more common. Until a 1962 Supreme Court ruling, many public schools required students to say Christian prayers in the morning. Today, teens are growing up in a culture in which many people say "Happy Holidays" instead of "Merry Christmas" to acknowledge that Christmas is not celebrated by everyone. Many schools today make accommodations for students who are not Christian, scheduling days off on Jewish holidays such as Yom Kippur and providing spaces for Muslim students to say their daily prayers.

suburbs: bedrooms they didn't have to share; basement rec rooms; the back seat of the family Buick. The opportunities to have sex were everywhere."[13] However, teens who "went too far" faced condemnation. A double standard meant that boys had more sexual freedom than girls, and girls were considered responsible for saying no.

But then, in the 1960s and 1970s, the sexual revolution made sex outside of marriage more socially acceptable. Contributing to this was a new development: the birth control pill. Sex education programs began. However, the double standard did not disappear. Sexual harassment—or unwanted sexual advances or behavior, often in the workplace—was seen as something women had to tolerate.

In the 1980s, the sexual revolution slowed down, largely because of the acquired immunodeficiency syndrome (AIDS) epidemic. In this more conservative decade, many schools taught "abstinence only" sex education. Research has shown that the resulting lack of knowledge about sex and birth control contributed to skyrocketing teen pregnancy rates.

The teen pregnancy trend reversed in the 1990s and 2000s for a number of reasons, including public health campaigns such as the National Campaign to Prevent Teen and Unplanned Pregnancy in 1996, which provided funding for sex education and access to contraception. The 1990s also saw a shift in attitudes about consent. The phrase *no means no* became popular, which questioned the assumption that if a girl says no to sexual activity, a boy should push for a yes.

Today's sexual attitudes have been shaped by the #MeToo movement that started in 2016, when thousands of women began to share on social media their experiences of being sexually assaulted or harassed. Teens today learn about enthusiastic or affirmative consent, which the Rape, Abuse & Incest National Network website defines as "looking for the presence of a 'yes' rather than the absence of a 'no.'"[14]

Political Awareness

Teen attitudes about politics have also shifted over time. Although youth activism was uncommon during the conservative 1950s and early 1960s, some young people joined the civil rights movement. In 1960, a group of Black college students initiated sit-ins to protest racial discrimination. They quietly sat at segregated lunch counters in North Carolina, despite being denied service.

In the 1960s and 1970s, youth activism exploded, largely because of opposition to the Vietnam War. College campuses became the center of a massive protest movement. Sometimes students were attacked by police or the National Guard, such as at Kent State University in 1970, when four protesters were killed. Young people also got involved with social movements like women's liberation and the environmental movement.

Teens in the 1980s and 1990s tended to be less concerned with politics. There was no singular crisis to motivate them like Vietnam. However, some young people did protest issues, including South African apartheid (a system of institutionalized racial discrimination) in the late 1980s and the US military action against Iraq during the Gulf War in 1991.

"This is a generation that's dealt with more trauma more quickly than any generation in 70 years."[15]

—John Della Volpe, youth and politics expert

Many teens today are more politically involved because they feel their lives have been impacted directly by politics. They are growing up with the threat of school shootings, climate change, and increased political violence. Their childhoods were impacted by COVID-19 lockdowns and mental health struggles. "This is a generation that's dealt with more trauma more quickly than any generation in 70 years,"[15] explains youth and politics expert John Della Volpe.

In response to fears about school shootings, many teens have been active in the fight for stricter gun legislation. For example, in 2018, after a deadly school shooting in Parkland, Florida, thousands of teens organized the March for Our Lives in Washington, DC, to demand gun regulations. Similarly, young people con-

Teens today are often politically involved. Here, teens protest gun violence at the March for Our Lives in Washington, DC, on March 24, 2018.

cerned about climate change have gotten involved in climate activism, including youth-led organizations such as Zero Hour, which organizes marches and educational campaigns. Many teens also participated in protests against police violence after the murder of George Floyd in 2020. Others demonstrated against the Israeli government and in support of Palestinian civilians during the Israel-Hamas war in 2024.

Teen culture changes over time in response to societal attitudes. In some ways, today's teens are different from previous generations—like today's revolution in how gender is understood. In other ways—like social activism—today's teens are not so different. Years from now, the people who are teens today might look back and compare themselves to the new generation of teens.

CHAPTER TWO

Socializing and Hanging Out

One of the main purposes of teen culture is to allow young people to develop identities independent from their parents. Teens do this in part by socializing with their peers. Although teens today socialize in different ways than their parents and grandparents did, there are also similarities. Teens seek out social spaces that are separate from the world of their parents—and that sometimes meet with parents' disapproval.

Perhaps most importantly, teens look for ways to have fun. Young people face all kinds of challenges—schoolwork, mental health, bullying, and so much more. But being a teenager can also be incredibly fun, and for many teens, socializing with peers is the most fun part.

Grandparents as Teens: Unscheduled Fun

Many of today's teens are accustomed to busy lives that are heavily scheduled with extracurricular activities, part-time jobs, and challenging classes. This is different from the way most teens' grandparents lived when they were young. Schoolwork tended to be less demanding. Although teens were involved in extracurricular activities, these typically did not dominate their time. Although some teens worked—especially if they came from poorer families or lived on farms—teens in this economically prosperous era were less likely to work than teens today. This meant that many teens had plenty of time on their hands to simply have fun. Their parents, who grew up in the challenging years of the Great Depression and World War II, did not always approve.

For children and younger teens, free time was spent socializing in their neighborhoods in unscheduled and largely unsupervised ways. During the post–World War II baby boom, neighborhoods were full of kids who hung out together. Outside, kids played games like marbles, tag, and hopscotch. Inside, they played board games like Monopoly and Yahtzee and with toys like Play-Doh, Lincoln Logs, and doll houses. Kids had freedom to explore on their bikes, and city kids rode buses or walked to places like movie theaters and candy stores. For older teens, the fun continued away from their neighborhoods once they had access to cars. "In the last half of the 1950s, nearly every teenager either had or could get the use of a car," recalls writer Tom Rodriguez. "As a result, no generation of teenagers ever had more opportunities to be alone with each other."[16]

When the grandparents of today's teens were young, they enjoyed a lot of unscheduled and unsupervised time in their neighborhoods. Many young children explored on their bikes, as shown in this photo from the 1970s.

Hangouts

With so many teens spending time away from their parents, the teen hangout became a phenomenon. "Teens have to have a place that's theirs. A place where there are no adult restrictions and everything is done their way," explains psychology professor Chator Mason. "In a way, the hangout is like a religious sanctuary. And in this sanctuary, ideas are swapped and social interaction takes place."[17]

Teen hangouts in the 1950s included restaurants—typically locally owned diners and soda shops, which sold inexpensive food like burgers and milkshakes. Many of these restaurants featured jukeboxes, which played records when teens put coins in them. Other hangouts included bowling alleys, roller-skating rinks, and miniature golf courses. Some of the most popular hangouts involved cars, including drive-in movie theaters and drive-in restaurants. Many parents bemoaned that the streets themselves were hangouts, with carloads of teens cruising down their local Main Street and downtown. In some cases, much to their parents' horror, they drag raced.

> "Teens have to have a place that's theirs. A place where there are no adult restrictions and everything is done their way."[17]
>
> —Chator Mason, psychology professor

Teens and Dancing

When rock and roll became extremely popular in the 1950s, so did dancing. For some teens, it was a joyful activity that allowed teens to express themselves during a conformist era. "What I remember most about the 50s were rules. Rules, rules, rules . . . for everything," writes John McKeon. "The *dance* rules were different. Dance with girls and hold this hand, but then . . . you could do whatever you wanted to do! Dance looked like freedom. The only freedom this kid knew."[18]

Since rock and roll was different from other forms of music, it required new dances like the twist, the hand jive, and the mashed potato. The dance crazes of the 1950s and 1960s spread after the television show *American Bandstand* started airing in 1957, which featured teens dancing to the latest hits. Although all the

The Roller Rink as Teen Hangout

Indoor roller-skating rinks started to become popular teen hangouts in the 1950s, and they reached peak popularity in the 1970s and 1980s. Roller rinks combined popular elements of other teen hangouts and gatherings. Like many teen hangouts, music was an essential part of the experience, with teens skating to a soundtrack of popular songs. Roller rinks also resembled sock hops and other dances because they centered on a fun physical activity. They also often featured a version of slow dancing called "slow skating," where couples skated hand-in-hand to romantic songs. In addition, like other teen hangouts, roller rinks gave teens the opportunity to socialize over food at the concession stand. In the 1980s, many roller rinks became part arcade as well, with video games and activities such as Skee-Ball. Roller rinks are still around, but these days many of the customers are baby boomers and Gen Xers skating together on nostalgia nights.

teens on the show were White, the show popularized the music of Black performers, along with dance steps that originated in the Black community.

Nervous about rock and roll and these new dances, adults exercised control by organizing school dances. Often these dances were held in gymnasiums and called "sock hops" because teens had to remove their shoes to avoid scuffing the floor.

Socializing in the 1980s and 1990s

In the 1980s and 1990s, the lives of some teens became more scheduled. Traveling sports leagues for both boys and girls became popular, especially in the 1990s, which is where the term *soccer mom* came from, describing parents driving their kids to soccer in their minivans. More children and young teens went to summer day camps. As the booming postwar economy became a distant memory, more teens were busy with part-time jobs.

At the same time, many teens during the 1980s and 1990s were even less supervised than their parents had been. Many kids and younger teens still socialized and rode bikes in their neighborhoods. The difference was that in the 1950s and 1960s, many women were not in the workplace, so there was at least some supervision from nearby mothers. In the 1980s and 1990s, many children and teens were "latchkey kids" who let themselves into empty homes after school. On top of that, divorce rates were at an all-time high, leaving kids to emotionally navigate difficult situations without much guidance.

Many people who grew up during this period fondly recall the freedom to socialize outside the view of their parents. "No adult in our face—watching, approving, organizing, structuring, or supervising every single thing we did," recalls Melissa L. Fenton, who grew up in the 1980s. "Every decision we made about how to spend our free time, *we* made."[19] Author Danielle Henderson also remembers this freedom fondly, albeit with reservations. "The hardest thing to convey to the children in my life about my childhood is the concept of unadulterated freedom," says Henderson, adding that "the 1980s were a decade of neglect, and I haven't felt freedom or terror like it since."[20]

Other teens who grew up during this era recall the bullying that came with lack of adult supervision. "People weren't just insensitive then," explains Trista, who grew up in the 1980s. "They didn't just lack cultural awareness and training. They were straight-up cruel and had no reservations about saying the meanest things that they could come up with." Moreover, many schools did not take bullying seriously. "Everyone assumed that a healthy dose of trauma was good for child development, and the best advice you could get was that boys would be boys,"[21] says Trista.

Teen Hangouts in the 1980s and 1990s

Like the grandparents of today's teens, the parents of today's teens also had hangouts where they could socialize in the absence of their parents. But for many teens, these hangouts reflected the mass commercialization of America. In the 1950s, teens hung out at small businesses like soda shops and drive-in theaters. By the 1980s, the American landscape was dominated by big chains. Many teens hung out at fast-food places such as Burger King, Taco Bell, Wendy's, Pizza Hut, and especially McDonald's, which reached peak popularity in the 1990s. In the mid-1990s, teens also started hanging out at coffee shops—sometimes at local ones, but more commonly at Starbucks, which had over two thousand US stores by 1999.

One feature of American life that peaked in the 1980s and 1990s was the shopping mall—and this was very much reflected in teen culture. The local Main Streets where teens congregated in the 1950s were replaced by malls, where many teens spent a great deal of time. "The mall was a sacred space," writes journalist Lisa Wong Macabasco. "It was where I got my hair and makeup done before prom, opened my first bank account, purchased my first prized pair of flare jeans, and nonchalantly surveilled my crush working at Hot Dog on a Stick. It was where teen life happened."[22] Teens shopped at record stores such as Sam Goody and inexpensive clothing stores such as Rave and Fashion Bug. They ate Sbarro pizza and drank Orange Juliuses at neon-lit food courts. Teens also congregated at mall arcades, especially in the early 1980s, where they saved their quarters to play *Pac-Man, Donkey Kong,* and *Dig Dug.*

Young people play a shooting game in an arcade. During the 1980s and 1990s, many teens had a lot of freedom to socialize away from their parents.

Video Games and Teen Culture

Since the early 1980s, video games have played an important role in teen culture for many young people. Teens were introduced to games such as *Pac-Man* and *Space Invaders* at mall arcades. Thanks to the Atari 2600 and the Commodore 64 home video consoles (which look primitive now, but were a big deal in 1982), teens started spending hours socializing together as they played video games. Consoles became more sophisticated, with the release of updated versions of Xbox, Nintendo, and Sony PlayStation consoles throughout the decades. Starting in the 1990s, multiplayer online games—including the very popular *World of Warcraft* in the mid-2000s—allowed teens to game with others remotely.

Today, according to a 2024 Pew Research Center study, 72 percent of teens who play video games are motivated to do so because it is a social experience. Of course, like all forms of teen hangouts, many adults have been suspicious of video games since they became popular. Over the years, countless print and online articles have fueled parents' fears about the effects of video games, especially violent ones. This is despite the fact that most research does not show a direct correlation between kids playing violent video games and kids committing real violence.

Socialization and Today's Teens

As a whole, teens today have less unscheduled free time than their parents had. Many are overscheduled with extracurricular activities, jobs, and challenging classes. Teens still socialize, but often this happens as a part of school activities. In addition, teens tend to be closer to their parents than teens were in previous generations. There are a number of reasons for this, including changing societal expectations about what it means to be an active parent. In addition, in some families, bonds between teens and their parents strengthened during the COVID-19 pandemic because they spent so much time together.

These changes have advantages and disadvantages. Many teens lack the freedom to explore that their parents and grandparents had. They also lack unstructured time and feel overwhelmed with their schedules. However, many kids receive more emotional support and attention than their parents did, both at home and at school.

Social Media: The New Teen Hangout?

Just like their parents and grandparents did, teens still hang out in person. "In the 21st century, a teen is often seeking out and doing what teens have done for decades. Hanging out with other teens,"[23] writes Leslie Crawford of GreatSchools.org. They eat fast food and study together at coffee shops. Some still go to malls—or to thrift shops, which reflects growing environmental consciousness.

However, for many teens, the hangout of choice is social media. According to a 2023 Pew Research Center study, 93 percent of American teens are on social media at least several times a day, and about 46 percent say they use social media constantly. According to Pew, the most popular teen social media sites are YouTube, TikTok, Snapchat, and Instagram. Teens socialize by using direct messages (DMs), joining group chats, live streaming, posting information and photos, liking and commenting on others' posts,

Teens today socialize by using group chats, live streaming, posting information and photos, liking and commenting on other's posts, and playing online multiplayer games.

and playing online multiplayer games. As Pew concludes, "Social media has given teens the ability to instantly connect with others and share their lives through photos, videos and status updates. Teens themselves describe these platforms as a key tool for connecting and maintaining relationships, being creative, and learning more about the world."[24]

> "Social media has given teens the ability to instantly connect with others and share their lives through photos, videos and status updates."[24]
>
> —Pew Research Center

Different as it is, social media shares similarities with teen hangouts from the past. Like other teen hangouts, social media is a space where teens can hang out independent of their parents and have fun. Also, just as parents were suspicious of teen hangouts in the past, many parents are suspicious of what teens are doing online. Newspapers, websites, and other media are filled with warnings about online dangers, including cyberbullying; online predators; and the impact that filtered, curated images of influencers who appear to have perfect lives have on the self-esteem and body image of teens.

According to the Pew Research Center study, teens are aware of these issues, and many share some of their parents' concerns. However, the study found that most teens think social media does more good than harm, primarily because it allows them to socialize. "Social media has definitely had some negative influence on me, but overall, it has been an overwhelmingly positive effect," says one girl who was interviewed for the study. "It allows me to connect with my friends in ways that would otherwise be impossible."[25]

Throughout the years, teen hangouts have shifted from soda shops to shopping malls to Snapchat. But the function of the teen hangout has not changed. Since the 1950s, when teens first had access to cars and the ability to gather away from their parents' eyes, teens have created spaces for themselves to socialize, develop identities of their own, and have fun.

CHAPTER THREE

Music and Teen Culture

Barbara Lane, a teenager in the 1960s, had a traumatic childhood in an abusive foster home. Pop music was her lifeline. "The music and lyrics of our day helped me maintain hope and a sense of determination that eventually I would get out of the nightmare I lived in," writes Lane. "The radical nature of songs written by artists such as Bob Dylan spoke to me. 'The Times, They Are a-Changing' gave me the courage to know I could change things for myself."[26]

Since the 1950s, popular music has been the soundtrack to the lives of countless teens as they explore their identities and navigate the challenges of youth. Although musical styles have changed, the importance of music to teen culture has not.

The 1950s: Rock and Roll

Rock and roll music is characterized by the use of electric guitars, drums, and danceable beats. Many parents were uncomfortable with those beats—and some White parents were uncomfortable because rock music was clearly influenced by genres that were popular in the Black community, such as rhythm and blues, gospel, and jazz. As rock and roll slowly gained popularity in the early 1950s, the 1954 smash hit "Rock Around the Clock" by Bill Haley & His Comets brought rock firmly into the mainstream. One of the first major rock artists was Elvis Presley, a teen idol who made parents uncomfortable by gyrating his hips.

The powerful impact of rock and roll music on teen culture in the 1950s cannot be exaggerated. As writer Tom Rodriguez explains,

> Looking back, the one thing that best characterized the years from 1955 to 1960 was the music. More than anything else, it was the music that was central to the lifestyle of America's teenagers. Everything revolved around it. It was everywhere and teenagers listened to their music on small transistor radios, portable record players, car radios, at home, in their cars, parties, picnics, dances and on television. Rock 'N' Roll music was the engine that drove the Teenage Revolution.[27]

The 1960s: Protest Music and the British Invasion

As teen culture became more rebellious in the 1960s, so did the music. Artists such as Bob Dylan and Joan Baez popularized folk music, with lyrics calling for civil rights and cultural change. Another rebellious genre was psychedelic rock—popularized by bands such as Pink Floyd and the Doors—which challenged musical norms with experimental sounds and surreal lyrics.

> "Rock 'N' Roll music was the engine that drove the Teenage Revolution."[27]
>
> —Tom Rodriguez, a writer who grew up during the 1950s

The 1960s also brought the British Invasion, popularizing British bands such as the Rolling Stones, the Who, and especially the Beatles, who became hugely famous after a 1964 television appearance on the *Ed Sullivan Show*. The Beatles became more countercultural throughout the 1960s, as cheerful melodies like "I Wanna Hold Your Hand" (1964) gave way to songs like "While My Guitar Weeps" (1968), which addressed the political and social upheaval of the era.

Many teens in the 1960s also listened to the Motown sound, the signature style of the Motown Records label. Motown featured Black performers and produced soulful, catchy music that played

The Beatles, shown here performing in 1964 on the Ed Sullivan Show, *became extremely popular among teens during the 1960s.*

a significant role in the racial integration of popular music. Popular Motown artists included Diana Ross and the Supremes, Marvin Gaye, Stevie Wonder, and Smokey Robinson.

The 1970s: Less Politics, More Mellow

Reflecting the less political decade of the 1970s, music tended to be less political than it was in the 1960s. Olivia Newton John's song "Have You Never Been Mellow" (1975) echoed the popular sentiment that it was time to relax. Many teens listened to soft-rock artists, including Elton John, Carly Simon, and James Taylor, and flamboyant glam-rock artists such as David Bowie and T. Rex.

In the late 1970s, many teens gravitated to disco, a style of music that emerged in Black, Latino, and LGBTQ clubs and became wildly popular after John Travolta played a rebellious young disco dancer in the movie *Saturday Night Fever* (1977). Disco featured rhythmic drum patterns, orchestral instruments, and sexy lyrics. Popular disco artists included Donna Summer, the Bee Gees, and the Village People. Disco dancing included synchronized dance moves such as the hustle and the electric slide, and the signature disco finger point that was popularized by Travolta. Although some teens despised disco—leading to a widespread debate about whether rock or disco was superior—others flocked to teen nights at discotheques in cities like New York.

While some teens were getting their disco groove on, others were finding an alternative community in the punk movement—an exception to the apolitical ethos of 1970s music. Punk music—including bands such as the Sex Pistols and the Ramones—has a raw and rebellious sound with antiestablishment lyrics. The punk community was known for do-it-yourself fashion—like leather jackets adorned with safety pins and band patches—and unconventional hairstyles, particularly brightly colored mohawks.

The 1980s: Teens Just Want to Have Fun

Popular music continued to be fun and not too serious in the 1980s—and also unique and a little wacky. "The Eighties are one of the weirdest eras ever for music," writes Rob Sheffield of *Rolling Stone* magazine. "It's a decade of excess. . . . It's got big hair, big drums, big shoulder pads. . . . Music gets louder, crazier, messier. Do you know where you are? You're in the Eighties, baby."[28]

The pop music of the 1980s was vibrant, punctuated with futuristic synthesizer music and larger-than-life artists. These artists were featured on MTV, a network that launched in 1981 to showcase music videos—a new phenomenon that teens gathered eagerly to watch. Artists were encouraged to play up their colorful dress and personas because this looked good on television.

Arguably the most successful artist of the MTV era, Michael Jackson dazzled teens with his sequined gloves and dance moves, especially the moonwalk. His smash 1982 hit album *Thriller* produced iconic videos, including those for "Beat It" (featuring choreographed gang members in a fight) and "Thriller" (featuring choreographed zombies in a graveyard.) Another MTV-friendly artist, Madonna, entertained teens with sexually provocative videos and her distinctive look—which inspired teenage girls to wear lace gloves, layered jewelry, and oversized hair bows. Cyndi Lauper, another popular and eccentric artist, donned neon hair and mismatched clothing as she fought with her amusingly oppressive father in the 1983 video to "Girls Just Want to Have Fun."

But there was more to 1980s music than just pop. Some teens listened to a new generation of rock with artists such as Bon Jovi and Van Halen, who were more polished than artists in the 1960s and 1970s and incorporated synthesizers and dramatic electric guitar solos. Other teens gravitated to heavy metal artists, particularly Metallica and Iron Maiden, or to more pop-friendly "glam metal" by bands such as Def Leppard and Mötley Crue. Others were inspired by new wave bands—including the Pet Shop Boys, New Order, and Erasure—who sang introspective lyrics and played synthesizer-heavy electronic music. The 1980s also saw the emergence of hip hop into mainstream culture, providing teens with social commentary from bands such as Public Enemy and N.W.A. as well as more lighthearted fare such as DJ Jazzy Jeff & the Fresh Prince's "Parents Just Don't Understand" (1988).

The 1990s and 2000s: Change, Angst, and Serious Issues

As writer Karen Johnson recalls, millennial teens experienced a lot of firsts and lasts. She writes, "Nineties kids were the last who had to memorize phone numbers. And remember directions. Or learn

Pop Punk

From the mid-1990s through the 2000s, another new genre emerged that gave teens an outlet for their angst: pop punk. Pop punk blends the fast-paced, rebellious spirit of punk with catchy melodies and hooks. Unlike traditional punk, pop punk is less focused on antiestablishment tropes and more focused on everyday life and relationship issues—with a special focus on teen struggles. Green Day, one of the first popular pop punk bands, attracted young fans with songs such as "Basket Case" (1994) and "American Idiot" (2004), which focused on defying social expectations. Other popular pop punk artists included Blink-182, Fall Out Boy, Paramore, New Found Glory, Sum 41, and Bowling for Soup. Pop punk has had a resurgence in the 2020s with artists such as Yungblud and Willow and with new albums by classic punk pop bands such as Fall Out Boy and Green Day.

to use maps." Yet at the same time, "nineties teens were the guinea pigs—the kids who 21st-century technology was initially exposed to."[29]

As teens navigated these transitions, there was plenty of angsty music to set the mood. In the early 1990s, a new genre called grunge emerged from Seattle, with artists such as Pearl Jam, Soundgarden, and especially Nirvana. Grunge is characterized by its raw, distorted guitar sounds, heavy drumming, and angry lyrics. Nirvana's "Smells Like Teen Spirit" (1991), which spoke to the disillusionment and boredom of being a teen, became an anthem of the 1990s.

Another angsty trend was the growing popularity of alternative or "indie" music. One well-known indie band was R.E.M., with songs such as "Losing My Religion" (1991) and "Everybody Hurts" (1992), which resonated with emotional teens. Other well-known indie groups included Radiohead, Smashing Pumpkins, Coldplay, Arcade Fire, and the Killers. One notable female artist was Tori Amos, who appealed to teen girls with personal songs—including "Me and a Gun" (1991), an a capella song that describes her experience being raped. To increase recognition for female artists, singer-songwriter Sarah McLachlan organized the Lilith Fair, a music festival that debuted in 1997 and exclusively featured female artists, including Jewel, Indigo Girls, and Tracy Chapman.

Considered by many to be the heyday of hip hop, the 1990s and 2000s produced hip hop that was political and dealt with social issues. With songs such as "Changes" (1998), which dealt with racism and police brutality, Tupac Shakur became an influential voice that resonated with many young people. Similarly political hip hop artists included Nas, Mos Def, and Lauryn Hill.

The 1990s and 2000s: Eclectic Pop

There was more to the 1990s and 2000s than angst. Some of the most popular music was soulful hip hop (such as Snoop Dogg and Coolio) and rhythm and blues (such as Usher and Boys II Men.) These genres included many female artists, such as the girl group Destiny's Child, whose lead singer, Beyoncé Knowles, became a megastar. Other popular girl groups included En Vogue and TLC, and iconic solo artists included Mariah Carey, Jennifer Lopez, and Brandy.

One genre of pop music aimed directly at teens was the boy band. Groups such as N'Sync and the Backstreet Boys counteracted the angst of grunge with catchy tunes and synchronized dance moves. In the late 1990s and early 2000s, similarly lighthearted music from young female artists, such as Britney Spears and Christina Aguilera, dominated the pop world.

Music with a party theme was also popular, including music from Latin artists such as Ricky Martin and Lou Bega. In the 2000s, electronic dance music became popular at dance clubs and crossed over to the mainstream.

Teen Culture and Pop Music Today

In the 1950s, there were fewer artists and fewer songs than there are today. The playlist of teens was generally whatever was on the radio, which was controlled by music industry gatekeepers and radio disc jockeys (DJs).

Teens today have access to a wide range of different musical options. However, megastars exist, like Taylor Swift, pictured performing in Chicago in June 2023.

Taylor Swift

The popularity of singer-songwriter Taylor Swift is staggering, especially among women and girls. With eleven albums since her debut in 2006, Swift is the world's first billionaire who was able to make a fortune almost entirely from music. As of May 2024, she is Spotify's most streamed artist of all time, and her 2024 album *The Tortured Poets Department* set a record with over 300 million streams on its first day. During her worldwide 2023–2024 Eras Tour—the highest-grossing tour of all time—her fans (or "Swifties") turned her shows into cultural events. They dressed up in costumes inspired by Swift's musical eras and exchanged friendship bracelets with strangers. Swift's appeal to teenage girls is partly because she sings about girlhood—including the autobiographical songs she wrote as a teenager, such as "Fifteen" (2009), or the trilogy of songs about a teenage love triangle ("Betty," "August," and "Cardigan") on her 2020 *Folklore* album. But even though most of Swift's songs are not written about teenagers, almost all of them are partly autobiographical and feel like a page out of her diary, which makes her music very relatable to many girls.

Today, teens have access to a staggering amount of music. For one thing, there are countless available genres. Although there are megastars—such as Taylor Swift, Billie Eilish, Beyoncé, Bad Bunny, the Weeknd, and Olivia Rodrigo—there is not a singular sound that defines the 2020s. Instead, what defines the decade is access to endless styles and the ability to mix and match to create one's own sound.

This access is largely due to the streaming platforms Spotify and Apple Music. As of 2024, there were over 100 million songs available on Spotify. This includes music from 1950 through the present. Unlike teens in the 1950s, who listened to music that was radically different from their parents' music, it is not uncommon for today's teens to listen to music that their parents and grandparents listened to when they were young. Songs from different decades occasionally wind up on the Billboard Top 100 list—as did Fleetwood Mac's 1977 hit "Dreams," which debuted at number twenty-one on the 2020 chart after a TikTok of a man skateboarding to the song went viral.

There are still gatekeepers in the music industry, but their influence is limited. Teens discover music through peer recommendations or by hearing it on social media. "A lot of my friends have Spotify accounts, or like Apple Music accounts, and we can follow each other and see each other's playlists to see what each other are listening to,"[30] explains fourteen-year-old Maddie De-Weese from Oregon.

"A lot of my friends have Spotify accounts, or like Apple Music accounts, and we can follow each other and see each other's playlists to see what each other are listening to."[30]

—Maddie DeWeese, a fourteen-year-old from Oregon

Today's teens listen to music that is more inclusive than ever before. Streaming services offer songs from all over the world. Unlike in the past, openly LGBTQ artists such as Lil Nas X, Sam Smith, Janelle Monae, and Chappell Roan are very popular among young people. Some artists openly express their politics, such as in Macklemore's "Hind's Hall" (2024), which is a tribute to 2024's pro-Palestinian encampments on college campuses.

Lil Nas X is shown here at a June 2023 concert in Belgium. Openly LGBTQ artists like Lil Nas X are very popular today, unlike in the past.

Dylan Lanier, a high school junior from California, argues that this diversification of music is a revolution. He writes, "As our music becomes increasingly open to past legends, future stars, and a broader variety of musicians everywhere, it only serves to wonder if our civilization is experiencing not only a revolution in our access to music, but in our openness towards growth and the rise of different voices."[31]

Although teens experience music in ways that differ from past decades, music has been an important part of teen culture since the 1950s. Regardless of the type of music, young people have always used music as a soundtrack to navigate their teen years.

CHAPTER FOUR

Television, Movies, and Teen Culture

In the 1950s, television networks and movie studios were instrumental in helping create a distinct teen culture. Their motivation to do so was financial. If teens were a separate demographic group, that meant they had a new market for their products. As a result, the television and movie industries have created content specifically for teens since that time. This content has become an essential part of teen culture.

Television in Postwar America

Television become wildly popular in the 1950s. According to media historian David Buckingham, the number of American households with a television grew from under 10 percent in 1950 to over 90 percent in 1965. By the mid-1950s, the average television set was on more than five hours a day.

In the early days, many teens watched television along with their families. This was because television was new and a novelty. Most people only had access to the three major networks—NBC, ABC, and CBS—and only for limited hours. For teens, hanging out with parents may not have been exciting, but television was.

For the most part, television in the 1950s and 1960s influenced teen culture by reinforcing traditional values. This

Two teenagers watch television in the 1950s. By the mid-1950s, television had become a popular form of teen entertainment, and the average television set was on more than five hours a day.

is because of television's business model. Networks sought to attract advertisers with large audiences—and the best way to attract a large audience is through uncontroversial content. The most popular television programs in the 1950s and 1960s were sitcoms about traditional families in which the mother stayed home and the father worked, such as *Father Knows Best* (1954–1960) and *I Love Lucy* (1951–1957).

Television and the Postwar Teen Market

To reach the teen market, television studios created teen dance shows. The most popular of these was *American Bandstand* (1952–1989), which was broadcast nationally. Many local markets broadcast local dance shows that aired during after-school hours. Although most of these programs featured all-White dancers, some local markets, such as Raleigh, North Carolina, aired dance shows with Black DJs and dancers. Similarly, in the 1960s, networks created teen shows about bands, such as *The Monkees* (1966–1968), which featured a real-life band by the same name that was developed specifically for the show.

In the 1960s, shows about teen characters were common. The first of these, *The Many Loves of Dobie Gillis* (1959–1963), focused on the romantic misadventures of a shy teenage boy. Some teen shows were about beach life and surfing, including *Gidget* (1965–1966), a lighthearted portrayal of a perky teen surfer girl. Although the spunky portrayal of Gidget made her acceptable for mainstream television, teen girls were drawn to the portrayal of a girl who defied gender roles by surfing. "The title character was an inspiration at a time when girls like me were growing up without many assertive role models," recalls journalist Delia O'Hara. "Gidget was spunky and intense, and she made me want to get out there and pursue my dreams."[32]

Movies and Postwar Teens

Whereas television in postwar America was often a family activity, teens watched movies with each other. Movie theaters, including drive-ins, were common hangout spaces for teens. Movies exposed teens to new ideas in a way that television did not because their longer format allowed for more thought-provoking plotlines. As a result, many parents were nervous about the impact of movies on their kids.

In the 1950s, films about so-called juvenile delinquents became popular. With titles such as *High School Hellcats* (1958) and *The Violent Years* (1956), these films reflected adult fears about nonconformist kids. These films were written about teens but were not written for them—with the exception of *Rebel Without a Cause* (1955), one of the most popular films of the decade. The film starred James Dean as a troubled teen who moves to a new town and befriends a pair of misfits. "One of the main things about *Rebel Without a Cause* is that it's not only a movie about teens, it's a movie that was made for them," explains writer Virginie Pronovost. "It shows an empathy towards them."[33] *Rebel Without a Cause* spoke to teens with an alternative narrative to the idyllic images of family life on television.

In the 1960s, films created for teens were abundant. On the lighter side, beach-themed movies such as *Beach Party* (1963) were a hit, along with various movies about surfer girl Gidget. Many teens flocked to horror movies, which included high-production classics such as Alfred Hitchcock's *Psycho* (1960) and low-budget flicks such as *Werewolf in a Girls' Dormitory* (1961). Others gravitated toward films about youth and rebellion, such as *The Graduate* (1967), a film about a young, disaffected man who has an affair with an older woman.

This picture shows a movie poster from the 1950s advertising Rebel Without a Cause, *starring James Dean. This was one of the most popular films of the decade because it was specifically made for teens.*

The Rocky Horror Picture Show

Since the late 1970s, many teens have participated in a unique cultural phenomenon centered around *The Rocky Horror Picture Show* (1975). The film itself is a campy horror story in the style of a musical, and the plot is about a couple who stumble upon a mad scientist who has created a muscular humanoid named Rocky. Although the film was initially a box office failure, it became a cult classic after theaters started midnight showings. Over time, viewers created an interactive, communal ritual while watching the film, complete with lots of audience participation. An unofficial "script" evolved for audiences, where they shouted out responses to lines in the film. People came to theaters dressed like the characters. In many theaters, regulars were asked to act out the film in front of the screen, using props that appeared in the film, like newspapers and toast. At the peak of the craze in the 1980s, hundreds of theaters around the country were hosting this ritual, and the movie continues to be shown in a limited number of theaters today.

Television and Teen Culture in the 1980s and 1990s

By the 1980s, television had become a significant part of teen life. According to several reports by Nielsen, an organization that measures television ratings, the average teen watched about twenty to twenty-four hours of television a week in the 1980s and 1990s. As blogger Canyon Walker recalls, keeping up with popular shows was an important part of teen culture. "After the airing of a really popular show, two-thirds or more of everybody in your peer group the next day had seen it and was excited to talk about it,"[34] he explains.

During this era, networks sought to reach the teen audience with realistic sitcoms and relatable teen characters. For example, *Family Ties* (1982–1989) focused on the generation gap between liberal parents and their conservative, materialistic kids and addressed issues like peer pressure and dating. Some of these shows were more diverse, including *The Cosby Show* (1984–1992) and *The Fresh Prince of Bel-Air* (1990–1996), which were about Black families with teen kids. Another popular show was *Saved by the Bell* (1989–1993), an upbeat show about a group of high school students.

Cable television became available in the 1980s, and teens flocked to music television network MTV. In the 1980s, MTV mostly showed music videos. Gradually, it switched to other teen programming, including the pioneering reality show *The Real World* (1994–present); crass teen cartoons such as *Beavis and Butt-Head* (1993–1997); and the brutally honest, documentary-style *16 and Pregnant* (2009–2014).

Teen Dramas

In the 1990s, teen dramas became a lucrative genre. Modeled after adult soap operas, these shows portray typical teen issues in angsty and sometimes melodramatic ways. "Teenagers really respond to what they like," explains Darren Star, producer of *Beverly Hills, 90210* and other teen dramas. "And they like to see something that says, 'I'm not alone.'"[35]

Popular teen dramas included *My So-Called Life* (1994–1995), *Dawson's Creek* (1998–2003), and *The O.C.* (2003–2007). But by far, the most iconic teen drama was *Beverly Hills, 90210* (1990–2000). The show centered on down-to-earth Minnesota teens Brenda and Brandon Walsh, who learn to adjust after moving to posh Beverly Hills. For many teens, *Beverly Hills, 90210* was mandatory watching to see whether brooding heartthrob Dylan would commit to his ex-girlfriend Brenda or to her best friend Kelly, or whether good girl Donna would graduate after being caught drunk at the prom.

> "Teenagers really respond to what they like. And they like to see something that says, 'I'm not alone.'"[35]
>
> —Darren Star, television producer

The Teen Movie Revolution

In the 1980s, teen audiences were treated to an explosion of realistic movies about teen life. Some of the most memorable of these films were directed by John Hughes. "[Hughes] had honorable messages: be true to yourself, reject oppressive authority, don't judge a book by its cover, live in the moment," writes film critic Lydia Smith. "And by teen movie standards, he spawned a revolution."[36] Hughes's films include *The Breakfast Club* (1985), a portrayal of five teens from different cliques who befriend each other during all-day detention at school, and *Ferris Bueller's Day Off* (1986), a comedy about an affable teen who skips school with his friends.

Teen films of the 1980s dealt with a number of themes, including romance. In an iconic scene in *Say Anything* (1989), love-lorn Lloyd Dobler serenades a girl with a boombox as he stands outside her window. Other films dealt with family issues, such as *Back to the Future* (1985), in which Marty McFly goes back in time and helps his parents grow into more confident adults. Bullying was also a common theme, such as in *The Karate Kid* (1984)*,* in which Daniel LaRusso learns karate to gain confidence and stand up to bullies. *Heathers* (1989) offers a darker take on the theme of bullies and cliques, as a dissatisfied popular girl and her rebel boyfriend murder the meanest popular kids in school.

Teens, Television, and Movies Today

Although today's teens do not watch as much television as their parents did, they are still watching. According to the media literacy organization Common Sense Media, 65 percent of tweens

Binge-Watching, Streaming Services, and Teens

One of the major differences in how today's teens watch television is binge-watching. Before streaming services took off in the mid-2000s, people generally watched television one episode at a time. After watching an episode, they had to wait a week for the next one to be broadcast. Starting in the 1990s, older television shows could be watched in their entirety on DVDs, but not new shows. Today, when streaming services release the new season of a show, they release all or a large portion of the season at one time. This means that viewers can watch—or binge-watch—a whole season in one sitting. For teens, binge-watching seasons has become a social experience. When a new season of a popular show is released, they gather together to watch the whole season. They also talk about the show on social media and create and comment upon videos that analyze characters and the plot. The downside to binge-watching is that, as the name implies, it has an addictive quality. On streaming services, when one episode ends, another automatically begins, which encourages viewers to continually watch one more episode.

and 49 percent of teens watch some form of television every day. The main difference today is in *how* teens watch television. Teens are more far likely to watch shows on their phones, tablets, or computers than on a television set. They also watch shows and clips of shows on YouTube. Broadpeak, a video streaming company, describes how young people watch television differently than their parents:

> Compared to prior generations, Gen Zers are more inclined to watch streaming services like Netflix rather than traditional television. They are also less committed TV watchers. They are more inclined to fast-forward through and only watch their favorite scenes or the most well-liked episodes. They prefer short-form videos and they are more prone to multitask while watching, often switching between different devices and screens at the same time.[37]

Teens today are more prone to multitask while using streaming services like Netflix, often switching back and forth between devices and screens.

Today's teens discuss television together, just as teens did in the past, and social media plays an important role in this. Teens give each other television recommendations on Instagram and TikTok. They also share YouTube playlists. Moreover, since around 2020, synchronized online watch parties have become increasingly popular with teens.

Teens also use streaming services to watch movies. According to the Motion Picture Association, about 18 percent of teens stream movies daily, and 60 percent do so at least once a week. Teens sometimes still go to movies as a social event with friends, especially when a blockbuster movie comes out that appeals to teens, such as *Barbie* in 2023. However, they are far less likely to see movies in theaters than their parents and grandparents were when they were young.

What Are Today's Teens Watching?

Just as there is no singular sound that defines the musical tastes of young people, there is no singular type of television show or movie. This is because of the huge variety of content available through streaming services and YouTube. Teens have access to shows and movies from different genres and can try new programming by watching a few scenes. This includes shows and movies from previous generations. Shows that were popular in the 1990s and 2000s have become popular among today's teens, including *Friends* (1994–2004), *Sex and the City* (1998–2004), and *The Office* (2005–2013).

Teen dramas remain popular, and many of these are available on streaming services. One of the most popular is *Never Have I Ever* (2020–2023), a coming-of-age story that follows Devi, a quirky Indian American high school student, along with her diverse group of friends. Some teen dramas are darker, such as *13 Reasons Why* (2017–2021), which focuses on a high school student's quest to discover why his classmate Hannah died by suicide, and *Euphoria* (2019–present), which addresses issues like addiction and mental illness through the struggles of seventeen-year-old Rue as she recovers from a drug overdose.

Other popular shows weave elements of teen drama with other genres. One of the all-time most-watched shows on Netflix is *Stranger Things* (2017–present), a story about teens and preteens in Hawkins, Indiana, in the 1980s. The characters navigate mysterious supernatural occurrences, government conspiracies, and a terrifying predatory monster called the Demogorgon. "Though the world of 'Stranger Things' is vastly different from society today, the characters aren't all that different from modern teenagers," explains pop culture writer Jordanna Garland. "Besides dealing with demogorgons and telekinetic powers, the characters of 'Stranger Things' display real emotions and experiences that come with being a teenager—dating, maintaining friendships, coming out and more."[38]

The Changing Role of Television and Film in Teen Culture

Since the 1950s, the television and film industries have been instrumental in defining the very concept of *teenager* by constructing teens as a lucrative marketing demographic. And, over the years, teens have gravitated to the content that has been created for them. From the drive-in theater of the 1950s to the virtual watch parties of today, teens have experienced television and movies together as a shared peer experience. Although the experience and the content of teen media over the years have changed, movies and especially television remain important parts of teen culture.

CHAPTER FIVE

Teen Fashion

Looking at photos of one's parents and grandparents as teens can be humorous. Everything looked so different—the clothes, the hair, the accessories. It might seem that when it comes to fashion, today's teens have little in common with their parents and grandparents.

However, even though styles change, the way fashion functions in teen culture stays the same. As teens explore their identities, fashion is a common way that teens express themselves. Teens sometimes choose fashion to fit in and sometimes to stand out. Generations of teens gravitate to styles and trends that differentiate them from their parents.

The 1950s: Conventional and Unconventional

In the conservative 1950s, many teens dressed in a conventional style known as the preppy look. "Preppy qualities were neatness, tidiness and grooming,"[39] explains Mike Palumbo, a lawyer who grew up in this era. Boys paired chino pants with polo shirts, button-down shirts, or argyle sweaters. They wore crew cuts or other short hairstyles.

> "Preppy qualities were neatness, tidiness and grooming."[39]
>
> —Mike Palumbo, a lawyer who grew up in the 1950s

For preppy girls, sweaters and modest skirts were typical—especially since most girls were not allowed to wear pants to school. Girls wore sweater sets—cardigan sweaters over matching short-sleeved tops—and blouses with prominent, rounded collars called Peter Pan collars. Girls wore full-flared circle skirts, sometimes emblazoned with a felt poodle, that always ended below the knee. Skirts were paired with saddle shoes—black-and-white shoes with a contrasting "saddle" in the middle—and ankle-length bobby socks worn with folded-down cuffs. Girls and boys both wore shoes called penny loafers that had a slit on top for displaying a coin.

Other teens dressed in unconventional ways that reflected the growing rebellious spirit of the decade. Inspired by movies such as *Rebel Without a Cause* (1955), boys wore leather jackets, white T-shirts, jeans, sunglasses, and black boots or Converse All-Stars. Boys wore eye-catching haircuts like the pompadour—short hair slicked back with pomade or petroleum jelly, with voluminous bangs elevated high above the forehead. Unconventional girls stretched the limits of school dress codes by wearing tight pencil skirts and sweaters. Away from school, they wore leather jackets and tight, cropped capri pants, along with bright red lipstick, winged eyeliner, and bandana hairbands.

Inspired by movies such as Rebel Without a Cause*, boys in the 1950s wore white T-shirts, black jeans, and black boots. They had haircuts like the pompadour— short hair slicked back with pomade or petroleum jelly, with voluminous bangs elevated high above the forehead.*

The 1960s: Mod and Hippie

While many teens continued to dress conservatively in the 1960s, others chose modern styles that broke sharply with tradition. One popular style was mod, a look that originated as high fashion in London and caught on with young American women and teens. According to fashion website Vintage Virtue, "Mod fashion encapsulated the spirit of a generation seeking to break free from the shackles of tradition. It was a rebellion against the conservative norms of the past, celebrating the dynamism and energy of youth culture."[40]

Unlike 1950s styles like full skirts and frilly Peter Pan collars, the mod look introduced sleek, minimal silhouettes, along with vivid colors and patterns. Girls wore miniskirts and shapeless short dresses called shift dresses. Short skirts were worn with knee-length go-go boots, which were made of vinyl or patent leather and came in bright colors. Girls also wore slim-fitting trousers—especially as more schools allowed girls to wear pants—and accessories like oversized sunglasses and colorful brooches. The boys' version of mod was largely inspired by the Beatles, with slim-fitting suit jackets worn over tight slacks or jeans. Boys wore mop-top hairstyles and newsboy caps.

Other teens adopted fashions influenced by the hippie movement. The hippie lifestyle centered around communal living, peace and love, and psychedelic music (and sometimes psychedelic drugs). To the shock of many parents, many boys emulated hippie style by growing their hair long. Both boys and girls wore tie-dyed clothing, moccasins, beaded jewelry, and clothing with peace sign emblems. Girls wore long bohemian skirts, fringed vests, peasant blouses, and handmade flower crowns.

The Bold 1970s

The bright colors and patterns popularized by the mod movement got even bolder in the 1970s—a loud and flamboyant decade for fashion. The color palette of the 1970s included avocado green, mustard yellow, hot pink, and lots of orange. Wild patterns were everywhere, including paisley, busy florals, and futuristic geometric designs. Thanks to disco in the late 1970s, fashion got even louder with disco-inspired shirts and dresses. These were made of shiny material, like satin or a metallic fabric called lamé. They came in bright shades, like purple or electric blue, and wild psychedelic patterns.

Style in the 1970s included a lot of hair. Many teen boys aspired to grow enough facial hair to have trendy enormous sideburns and long handlebar mustaches. Boys showed off chest hair by wearing partially unbuttoned tops. For girls, very straight long hair was in style, which some girls achieved by using an actual iron. Later in the decade, girls wore hair that was layered and feathered, inspired by actress Farrah Fawcett. For many Black

Wild patterns were common in teen fashion in the 1970s. Teens often wore tight-fitting clothing with bold stripes or wild floral patterns.

teens, wearing natural hair and eschewing straightening products was a sign of Black pride.

Bell-bottom pants were one of the most iconic fashions of the 1970s. Worn by both boys and girls, these flared pants were tight at the thighs and wide from the knees down. Girls decorated their bell-bottom jeans with iron-on patches, and they also wore bell-bottomed jumpsuits. They sometimes paired bell-bottoms with high, clunky platform shoes.

The Eclectic 1980s

The colorful and unconventional fashion aesthetic of the 1970s continued into the 1980s. "The 1980s was possibly the boldest decade in modern fashion history, a magical era of over-the-top silhouettes, teased perms and saturated colors," writes style reporter Marianna Cerini. "They were the years of puffed shoulders and power suits, flashy skirts and spandex leggings, velour, leg warmers and voluminous parachute pants."[41]

Teens in the 1980s got to choose from many unique trends. In the early 1980s, parachute pants were in style for both boys and girls. Made from shiny nylon or polyester, these baggy pants were adorned with nonfunctional zippers. Girls paired them with fluorescent sweatshirts or off-the-shoulder sweatshirts popularized by the movie *Flashdance* (1983). Other notable trends included leg warmers (inspired by the aerobics craze of the early 1980s), shoulder pads (inspired by fashion icon Princess Diana), armfuls of Swatch watches, and stonewashed jeans.

Stirrup pants were another distinctive trend. These stretchy cotton leggings had straps that looped around the bottom of the foot. Girls wore stirrup pants as part of a layered, color-coordinated look with oversized button-up shirts and matching accessories like tank tops, socks, and chunky jewelry. The look was typically tied together with a stretchy belt cinched over the shirt.

> "The 1980s was possibly the boldest decade in modern fashion history, a magical era of over-the-top silhouettes, teased perms and saturated colors."[41]
>
> —Marianna Cerini, style writer

Unique Accessory Trends from the 1970s and 1980s

The bold, unique fashions of the 1970s and 1980s were punctuated by some memorable accessories. In the 1970s, girls wore bulky rings called mood rings, which came with a rock that changed colors based on the wearer's mood (although there was no scientific evidence to back that up). In the late 1970s, digital watches—which display time numerically as opposed to on a clockface—were invented and became trendy accessories. In the 1980s, digital watches that also functioned as calculators became available. In the 1980s, the Rubik's Cube—an iconic six-sided puzzle—became available on a chain in necklace form. The cube on the necklace was fully functional and served as both an accessory and an amusement. The 1980s also saw trends inspired by Michael Jackson, including white gloves and fedora hats. There were also plenty of accessories inspired by Madonna, including large crucifix necklaces, mesh tops, oversized hair bows, and fingerless lace gloves. Jelly bracelets were another popular 1980s trend. These were colorful, flexible rubber bracelets that girls wore by the armful.

Hairstyles in the 1980s were dramatic. Many girls wore "big hair," a look created by using a hot curling iron, a hair pick, and hairspray. Big hair was adorned with accessories like scrunchies and banana clips, which were U-shaped clips that held hair in place and made it even bigger. For boys, two of the most memorable hairstyles were the mullet (short on the top and sides and long in the back) and the rat tail (short hair with a long, thin "tail' of hair).

The 1990s and 2000s: Minimalism and Grunge

Unlike the bold fashions of the 1970s and 1980s, teen fashion trends in the 1990s and 2000s were quieter and more low-maintenance. "As the 20th century came to a close, fashion reached its most casual," explains Karina Reddy of the Fashion History Timeline. "Women's fashion became more streamlined as minimalism became de rigueur."[42]

One of the most iconic casual looks of the 1990s was grunge, a rugged, unkempt look that originated in Seattle as part of the grunge music movement. Oversized flannel shirts were the most iconic staples of the grunge era, along with ripped jeans and combat boots. Other casual looks included oversized sweat-shirts, bucket hats, Keds sneakers, and slip dresses, which were basically just body slips with spaghetti straps. The big hairstyles of the 1980s gave way to simpler, straight styles, including "the Rachel"—a layered, face-framing haircut popularized by the character Rachel from *Friends*. In the late 1990s, hip hop and skater culture inspired an ultracasual look: teen boys wearing saggy pants that exposed their underwear. Predictably, parents were horrified.

Casual looks for teens continued to be popular throughout the 2000s. Jeans were very popular. At the beginning of the de-cade, low-rise jeans were very popular with girls, sometimes with back pockets bejeweled with rhinestones. This look was paired with cropped baby tees for maximum belly exposure. Later in the decade, more modest looks, like bootcut and skinny jeans, were popular. For boys, baggy jeans were in style, and both girls and boys bought jeans that came pre-torn and frayed. Other causal looks of the 2000s included tracksuits, graphic T-shirts, cargo pants, trucker hats, and colorful sneakers.

Today's Fashion: Maximum Casual

It's hard to look forward and predict what trends will be remem-bered as emblematic of the 2020s. But one trend that will likely be memorable is how casually many teens dress. The trend toward casual dress that started in the 1990s was amplified when teens were stuck at home during the COVID-19 pandemic. Teens wore pajamas and sweats for months; for many, ultracasual dressing continued as students went back to school.

Since the late 2010s, one of the most popular types of ca-sual clothing has been athleisure—comfortable, sporty clothing designed for working out but often worn as an everyday look.

Athleisure wear includes moisture-wicking T-shirts, tank tops, and track jackets. However, athleisure is associated most with bottoms, especially formfitting leggings made out of stretchy materials such as nylon and Lycra. Other athleisure bottoms include joggers, which are sweatpants that taper at the ankle, and yoga pants, which often are flared at the bottom. Although athleisure bottoms have not replaced jeans, these zipper-free casual pants have become a popular alternative.

Today's Fashion: Microtrends

Microtrends—or fashion trends that appear and disappear in a matter of months—are another defining aspect of today's teen fashion. Microtrends are fueled by social media. "The term microtrend refers to a specific article of clothing, makeup, or style that takes over algorithms (on TikTok, specifically) for short periods

Both body piercings and a wide range of different hair colors are common among teens today. Fashion that crosses the line between male and female is also more common than in the past, as gender roles are less rigid.

Fast Fashion Versus Thrifting

Two seemingly contradictory trends are popular among teens today: the frequent purchase of fast fashion and shopping at thrift stores. *Fast fashion* refers to inexpensive, trendy clothing that is quickly produced to keep up with the latest fashion trends. Microtrends have fueled the fast fashion industry because teens who want to keep up with the ever-changing trends need to shop often. Fast fashion is easily available to teens through in-person and online stores, where cheaply made, often low-quality clothing and accessories are available at enticingly low prices.

At the same time, many teens are eschewing fast fashion in favor of shopping at in-person and online thrift stores. Like fast fashion, thrifting appeals to teens because it is inexpensive. Teens can also sell unwanted clothing at both in-person and online thrift stores. For many teens, thrift stores represent a way to mitigate the environmental impact of fast fashion. They also represent a way for teens to express themselves through fashion in a more individualistic way than following microtrends.

of time, making teens think they need it, and then vanishes only so that we move on to the next," explains Soleil Richardson, a high school senior from Massachusetts. "Thanks to social media, the lifespan of fashion and beauty trends is getting shorter and shorter."[43] Endless microtrends have cycled through during the 2020s—including multicolored fishnet stockings under ripped jeans, old-fashioned "cottage core" dresses with puffed sleeves, cow-printed tops, silver heart pendants, "furry" purses, and so much more.

Critics of microtrends argue that this contributes to climate change by ramping up the production of clothing to keep up with trends. Others argue that teens are being manipulated by TikTok; many of the microtrend items promoted by the platform's algorithm are sold in the TikTok store. In contrast, others point out that with so many available microtrends, teens have a smorgasbord of looks to choose from to create their individual style.

> "Thanks to social media, the lifespan of fashion and beauty trends is getting shorter and shorter."[43]
>
> —Soleil Richardson, a high school senior from Massachusetts

Today's Fashion: Alternative Is the New Normal

Another attribute of 2020s fashion is that styles previously associated with "alternative" kids have become more accepted or mainstream. One of these trends is hair dye in colors like blue, pink, and purple. In the past, this kind of hair dye was associated with countercultural movements like the 1970s punk subculture. Today, experimenting with different hair colors has become typical for many teens, and brightly colored hair dyes are easy to find. Similarly, body piercings used to be countercultural (other than pierced earlobes for girls), and now many teens have piercings in their noses, belly buttons, or upper earlobes.

In addition, in an era in which transgender and gender-nonconforming teens are more accepted and gender roles are less rigid, fashion that crosses the line between male and female is more common. When the grandparents of today's teens were young, there were clear rules about what boys wore and what girls wore. Today, it is not uncommon to see boys wearing nail polish, makeup, or pink or floral-patterned clothes. Clothes that were once considered masculine, like oversized sweatshirts and sports jerseys, are more commonly seen as unisex.

Throughout the years, teens have expressed themselves through fashion. Sometimes these choices have reflected mainstream values; other times, teens have chosen fashions to challenge boundaries. The ever-evolving landscape of teen fashion serves as a mirror that reflects changing social norms and the creativity of youthful expression.

SOURCE NOTES

Introduction:
Teen Culture: Today and in the Past

1. Quoted in *Learning Network* (blog), "Teenagers on the Best Thing About Being Their Age," *New York Times,* April 27, 2023. www.nytimes.com.
2. Tom Rodriguez, "America's Teenage Revolution: 1955–1960," *Tom Rodriguez . . . Remembrances and Reflections of My Life* (blog), April 2, 2021. https://tomrodriguezlv.com.
3. Christine N., "15 Reasons Why Growing Up in the 1980s Was the Best," Houston Moms, August 1, 2019. https://houston mom.com.
4. Derek Thompson, "A Brief History of Teenagers," *Saturday Evening Post*, February 13, 2018. www.saturdayeveningpost .com.

Chapter One:
Changing Attitudes, Changing Times

5. Planned Parenthood, "What Are Gender Roles and Stereotypes?" www.plannedparenthood.org.
6. Karen Osburn, "Growing Up in the 1960s," *Historic Geneva Blog*, September 11, 2015. https://historicgeneva.org.
7. Heather Cumiskey, "Teens Today vs. 1980s: The Quest to Belong," *Heather Cumiskey* (blog). https://heathercumiskey.com.
8. Anna North, "The Past, Present, and Future of Body Image in America," Vox, October 18, 2021. www.vox.com.
9. Jean M. Twenge, "How Gen Z Changed Its Views on Gender," *Time*, May 1, 2023. https://time.com.
10. Digital Public Library of America, "Children in Progressive-Era America: Teenage Culture." https://dp.la.
11. Chris Lane, "Forget the Nostalgia: 7 Things About the 1980s That Sucked," *Houston Press*, August 4, 2016. www.houston press.com.
12. Quoted in Francesca Paris and Claire Cain Miller, "What It's Like to Be a Queer Teenager in America Today," *New York Times*, June 3, 2023. www.nytimes.com.
13. Gabrielle Glaser, "The Sexual Double Standards That Led to the Baby Boom—and 'Girls in Trouble,'" Literary Hub, January 27, 2021. https://lithub.com.

14. Rape, Abuse & Incest National Network, "What Consent Looks Like," October 30, 2020. https://rainn.org.
15. John Della Volpe, *Fight: How Gen Z Is Channeling Their Fear & Passion to Save America*. New York: St. Martin's, 2022.

Chapter Two:
Socializing and Hanging Out

16. Rodriguez, "America's Teenage Revolution."
17. Quoted in Erik Hamilton, "A Place to 'Hang': Rituals: From Soda Shops to Shopping Malls, Generations of Teens Have Been Searching for Somewhere to Be Themselves," *Los Angeles Times,* January 6, 1991. www.latimes.com.
18. Quoted in Richard Powers, "The Life of a 1950s Teenager." www.richardpowers.com.
19. Melissa L. Fenton, "9 Reasons Why Growing Up in the 80s Was Totally B*tchin'," Scary Mommy, March 4, 2021. www.scarymommy.com.
20. Danielle Henderson, "Those Were the Days of Our Lives," The Cut, July 14, 2021. www.thecut.com.
21. Trista, "Despite Your Love for *Stranger Things,* the '80s Actually Sucked, Here's Why," History Collection, September 16, 2019. https://historycollection.com.
22. Lisa Wong Macabasco, "An Illustrated Ode to the 1980s Shopping Mall, Through Teen Eyes," *Vogue*, February 27, 2024. www.vogue.com.
23. Leslie Crawford, "Where Teens Hang Out," GreatSchools.org, May 7, 2024. www.greatschools.org.
24. Monica Anderson, Emily A. Vogels, Andrew Perrin, and Lee Rainie, "What Teens Post on Social Media," Pew Research Center, November 16, 2022. www.pewresearch.org.
25. Quoted in Monica Anderson, Emily A. Vogels, Andrew Perrin, and Lee Rainie, "Teens' Views About Social Media," Pew Research Center, November 16, 2022. www.pewresearch.org.

Chapter Three:
Music and Teen Culture

26. Barbara Lane, "Radical Hope and Boomer Music," *Boomer*, October 4, 2023. www.boomermagazine.com.
27. Rodriguez, "America's Teenage Revolution."
28. Rob Sheffield, "The 200 Best Songs of the 1980s," *Rolling Stone*, November 23, 2023. www.rollingstone.com.

29. Karen Johnson, "Why I Loved Being a Teen in the 90s," Her View from Home. https://herviewfromhome.com.

30. Quoted in Crystal Ligori, Jenn Chavez, and Donald Orr, "From Tik-Tok to '80s Rock: Teens Walk Us Through What They're Listening To," Oregon Public Broadcasting, June 13, 2020. www.opb.org.

31. Dylan Lanier, "From a Teen's Perspective: The Music Revolution," InMenlo, March 6, 2023. https://inmenlo.com.

Chapter Four:
Television, Movies, and Teen Culture

32. Delia O'Hara, "My Role Model, Gidget," *Delia O'Hara* (blog), August 26, 2013. https://deliaohara.com.

33. Virginie Pronovost, "Being a Teenager in the 50s: 'Rebel Without a Cause' (Nicholas Ray, 1955)," *Wonderful World of Cinema* (blog), July 17, 2018. https://thewonderfulworldofcinema.wordpress.com.

34. Canyon Walker, "Another 5 Things About TV in the 1980s," *Tales of a Traveling Wiseguy* (blog), January 18, 2024. https://canyon walker.livejournal.com.

35. Quoted in Samantha Highfill, "For the Love of Teen TV: How the Genre Has Evolved and Why It's So Powerful," *Entertainment Weekly*, May 10, 2021. https://ew.com.

36. Lydia Smith, "The Evolution of the Teen Movie," Buffed Film Buffs, February 14, 2022. www.buffedfilmbuffs.com.

37. Broadpeak, "Youth's Watching Habits: How Is Gen Z Consuming Video?," May 15, 2024. https://broadpeak.tv.

38. Jordanna Garland, "'Stranger Things' and Its Resonance on Generation Z," *The Review*, August 16, 2022. https://udreview.com.

Chapter Five:
Teen Fashion

39. Mike Palumbo, "The Fifties' Teenage Phenomenon—Preppies, Greasers and Juvenile Delinquency," 20th Century History Song Book. https://20thcenturyhistorysongbook.com.

40. Vintage Virtue, "Fashion Revolution: The Bold and Innovative Trends of 1960s Mod Style." https://vintagevirtue.net.

41. Marianna Cerini, "'80s Fashion: Trends from the 'More Is More' Style Decade That Keep Coming Back," CNN, July 8, 2020. www.cnn.com.

42. Karina Reddy, "1990–1999," Fashion History Timeline, September 24, 2020. https://fashionhistory.fitnyc.edu.

43. Soleil Richardson, "Social Media Micro-Trends and the Consumerism Cycle," *The Willistonian*, April 7, 2024. www.willistonian.org.

FOR FURTHER RESEARCH

Books

Ilene English, *Hippie Chick: Coming of Age in the '60s.* Scottsdale, AZ: She Writes, 2019.

Thea Glassman, *Freaks, Gleeks, and Dawson's Creek: How Seven Teen Shows Transformed Television*. Philadelphia: Running, 2023.

James King, *Fast Times and Excellent Adventures: The Surprising History of the '80s Teen Movie.* London: Constable, 2018.

Chuck Klosterman, *The Nineties: A Book.* New York: Penguin, 2023.

Jon Savage, *Teenage: The Creation of Youth, 1875–1945.* London: Faber & Faber, 2021.

Nicholas Tochka, *Rocking in the Free World: Popular Music and the Politics of Freedom in Postwar America.* Oxford, UK: Oxford University Press, 2023.

Jean M. Twenge, *Generations: The Real Differences Between Gen Z, Millennials, Gen X, Boomers, and Silents, and What They Mean for America's Future.* New York: Atria, 2023.

Internet Sources

Richard Fisher, "Why Teenagers Aren't What They Used to Be," BBC, February 1, 2022. www.bbc.com.

Samantha Highfill, "For the Love of Teen TV: How the Genre Has Evolved and Why It's So Powerful," *Entertainment Weekly*, May 10, 2021. https://ew.com.

Learning Network (blog), "Teenagers on the Best Thing About Being Their Age," *New York Times,* April 27, 2023. www.nytimes.com.

Natalie Prouix, "What Is It Like to Be a Teenager Now?," *New York Times*, January 18, 2023. www.nytimes.com.

Derek Thompson, "A Brief History of Teenagers," *Saturday Evening Post*, February 13, 2018. www.saturdayeveningpost.com.

Jean M. Twenge, "How Gen Z Changed Its Views on Gender," *Time*, May 1, 2023. https://time.com.

ORGANIZATIONS AND WEBSITES

David Hoffman
www.youtube.com/channel/UC6wBro4B4pf9xnBh9Xi2zcQ
This is the YouTube channel of historical documentarian David Hoffman. Viewers can find hundreds of short videos—including in-depth personal interviews—about what it was like to grow up in the 1950s and 1960s.

Do You Remember?
https://doyouremember.com
This frequently updated website includes videos and stories about popular music, celebrities, and popular culture from the past and present. The site also includes pop culture polls such as "Who Is Your Favorite '70s TV Dad?" as well as nostalgia-based games and quizzes.

Fashion History Timeline
https://fashionhistory.fitnyc.edu
Hosted by the Fashion Institute of Technology in New York City, this website features detailed information and images of clothing trends from throughout history, including clothing trends from the years today's teens' parents and grandparents were growing up.

Nostalgia Machine
http://thenostalgiamachine.com
This website is a database of popular music videos and music clips since 1951. After users select a year, they are directed to a list of clickable music resources from that year.

Recollection Road
www.youtube.com/@RecollectionRoad
This YouTube video series includes detailed, colorful videos about American life since the 1950s, with an emphasis on teen culture, trends, gadgets, and popular culture.

INDEX

opinion polls. *See* surveys
Osburn, Karen, 9

Palumbo, Mike, 47
Pet Shop Boys, 31
Pew Research Center, 13, 14, 24, 25–26
Planned Parenthood, 8
political awareness/activism, 16–17
    music and, 27, 28
    in 1980s/1990s, 16
"political correctness," 13
polls. *See* surveys
pop punk, 31
prayer in schools, 14
pregnancy, teen, 15
Presley, Elvis, 27
Prince, 10
Pronovost, Virginie, 39–40
Psycho (film), 40
punk music, 30

racial discrimination/segregation, 11–12
protests against, 16
Ramones, 30
Rape, Abuse & Incest National Network
    (website), 15
Rebel Without a Cause (film), 39–40, 48
    poster for, **40**
Recollection Road (website), 61
Reddy, Karina, 52
R.E.M., 32
Richardson, Soleil, 54–55
rock and roll, 12
"Rock Around the Clock" (song), 27
Rocky Horror Picture Show, The (film), 41
Rodriguez, Tom, 4, 19, 28
roller-skating rinks, 21
Roper poll, 14

Saturday Night Fever (film), 29
Say Anything (film), 43
school shootings, 16–17
Sex and the City (TV program), 45
sex education, 15
    changing attitudes about, 14–15
Sex Pistols, 30
sexual revolution, 15
    AIDS epidemic and, 15
Shakur, Tupac, 32
Sheffield, Rob, 30
Sixteen Candles (film), 12
"Smells Like Teen Spirit" (song), 32
Smith, Lydia, 42
Snapchat, 25, 26
socializing/social spaces

in earlier generations, 18–19
    in 1980s/1990s, 21–22
social media, 25–26
Spears, Britney, 33
Spotify (streaming platform), 35
Stranger Things (TV program), 46
streaming platforms, 34
surveys
    on attitudes on premarital sex, 14
    on change in ethnic/racial diversity
        among teens, 13
    on religious affiliation, 14
    on social media use, 25, 26
    on teens identifying as LGBTQ, 13–14
    on teens' television viewing, 43–44
Swift, Taylor, **33**, 34

teenagers, concept as distinct
    demographic group, 5
teen culture
    post–World War II, 6
    today, 7
television
    binge-watching of, 43
    changing role in teen culture, 46
    gender roles reinforced by, 8
    MTV, 30
    of 1950–1960s, 37–39
    of 1980s–1990s, 41–42
    streaming, 44–45
"The Times, They Are a-Changing " (song),
    29
Tortured Poets Department, The (album),
    34
13 Reasons Why (TV program), 45
Thompson, Derek, 5
Thriller (album), 30
TikTok, 11, 25, 54–55
Twenge Jean M., 11

Van Halen, 31
Vietnam War protests, 6, 16
Vintage Virtue (website), 49
Violent Years, The (film), 39

Walker, Canyon, 41
Werewolf in a Girls' Dormitory (film), 40
What to Do on a Date (mental hygiene
    film), 11
"While My Guitar Weeps" (song), 28
"woke" concept, 13

YouTube, 45

Zero Hour, 17